PIANO · VOCAL · GUITAR

COUNTRY GOSPEL

ISBN 0-634-05479-1

HAL•LEONARD®
CORPORATION

7777 W. BLUEMOUND RD. P.O. BOX 13819 MILWAUKEE, WI 53213

Visit Hal Leonard Online at
www.halleonard.com

Contents

4	Are You Walkin' and A-Talkin' for the Lord
10	Church in the Wildwood
7	Crying in the Chapel
12	Family Bible
15	The First Step to Heaven
24	Give Me That Old Time Religion
26	He Turned the Water into Wine
34	A Home in Heaven
31	How Beautiful Heaven Must Be
36	I Feel Like Traveling On
38	I Know What Lies Ahead
46	I Saw the Light
49	I Wouldn't Take Nothing for My Journey Now
52	I'd Rather Be an Old Time Christian
60	I'll Fly Away
62	If Not for the Love of Christ
70	It Was Jesus
55	It's Heaven Calling Me
72	Just a Closer Walk with Thee
74	Just a Little Talk with Jesus
76	Land of Israel
84	Last Night I Dreamed of Heaven
86	Lead Me, Father
88	Life's Railway to Heaven
81	On the Jericho Road
90	One More Valley
93	Peace in the Valley
96	Precious Memories
102	Put Your Hand in the Hand
99	Ready to Go Home
106	Safely in the Arms of Jesus
109	Sheltered in the Arms of God
112	Show Me the Way to Go
118	Someone to Care
121	This Is Just What Heaven Means to Me
124	To My Mansion in the Sky
127	Turn Your Radio On
130	The Unclouded Day
132	Wealth Won't Save Your Soul
138	When the Book of Life Is Read
140	Where Could I Go
142	Who Am I
146	Why Me? (Why Me, Lord?)
135	Will the Circle Be Unbroken
148	Wings of a Dove

ARE YOU WALKIN' AND A-TALKIN' FOR THE LORD

Words and Music by
HANK WILLIAMS

6

CRYING IN THE CHAPEL

Words and Music by
ARTIE GLENN

Slowly, with expression

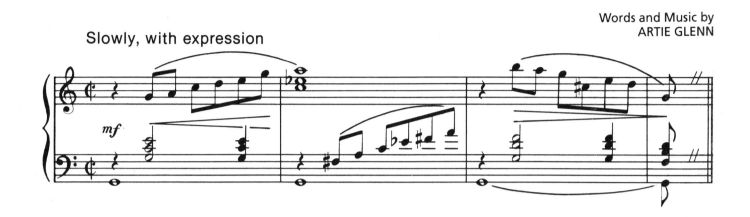

Chorus

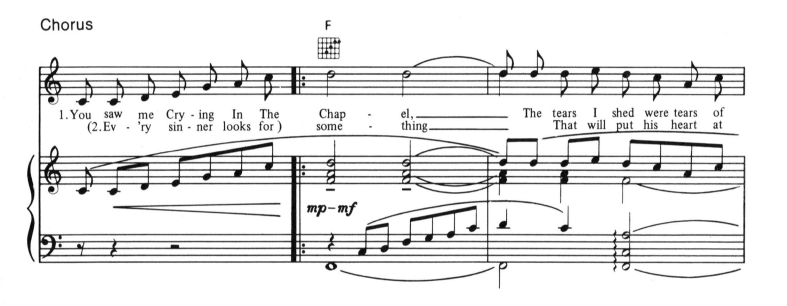

1. You saw me Cry-ing In The Chap-el, ____ The tears I shed were tears of
(2. Ev-'ry sin-ner looks for) some-thing ____ That will put his heart at

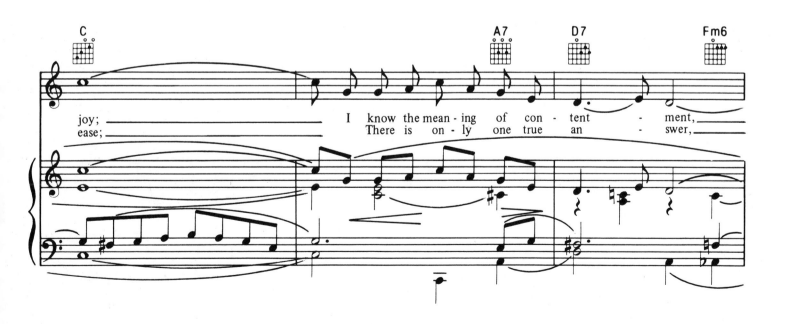

joy; ____ I know the mean-ing of con-tent-ment, ____
ease; ____ There is on-ly one true an-swer, ____

CHURCH IN THE WILDWOOD

Words and Music by
DR. WILLIAM S. PITTS

FAMILY BIBLE

Words and Music by WALT BREELAND,
CLAUDE GRAY and PAUL BUSKIRK

There's a fam - 'ly Bi - ble on the ta - ble,
end of day when work was o - ver,
world of ours is full of trou - ble,

its pag - es torn and hard to read.
and when the eve - ning meal is done,
but this world would oh, so bet - ter be

But the fam - 'ly Bi - ble on the ta - ble
Dad would read to us from the fam - 'ly Bi - ble,
if we had more Bi - bles on the ta - ble,

THE FIRST STEP TO HEAVEN

Words and Music by EMORY GORDY
and JIM RUSHING

Wake up, oh, sin - ner, you are fac - ing the dark - ness of death.

Each mo - ment could be the mo - ment you

draw your last ___ breath. ___

And the weight of your fears ___ are the shack - les that

keep you en - slaved. ___

But the blood of the Lamb_____ is the one way to

by - pass the grave.

The

The first step to heav - en is

first step to heav - en,

deeds.

A

man - sion up yon - der is re - served for those who be -

lieve.

The first step to

D.S. al Coda

GIVE ME THAT OLD TIME RELIGION

Traditional

3. It was good for old Abe Lincoln;
It was good for old Abe Lincoln.
It was good for old Abe Lincoln,
And it's good enough for me.

HE TURNED THE WATER INTO WINE

Words and Music by
JOHN R. CASH

HOW BEAUTIFUL HEAVEN MUST BE

Words by MRS. A.S. BRIDGEWATER
Music by A.P. BLAND

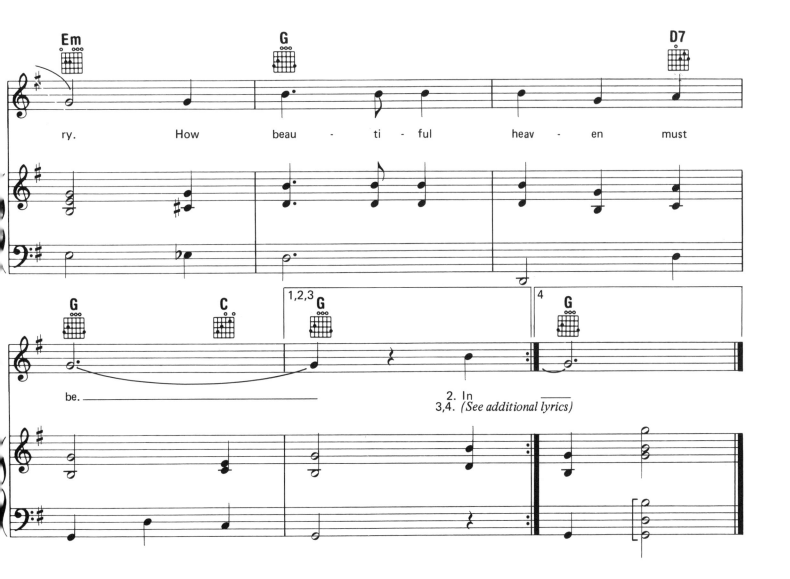

3. Pure waters of life there are flowing,
   And all who will drink may be free.
   Rare jewels of splendor are glowing.
   How beautiful heaven must be.

4. The angels so sweetly are singing,
   Where all is so happy and free.
   Sweet chords from their gold harps are ringing.
   How beautiful heaven must be.

A HOME IN HEAVEN

Words and Music by
HANK WILLIAMS

Moderately

A - round me man - y are build - ing
Long is the road ____ that leads you ____ to that
read - y for ____ His com - ing, ____

homes of beau - ty and wealth, ____ but
beau - ti - ful home ____ up there. ____ Is
have you been true all a - long? ____ Have you

what of a home in Heav - en? ____
work on your home com - plet - ed? ____
fin - ished your build - ing in Glo - ry, ____ will you

I FEEL LIKE TRAVELING ON

Words by WILLIAM HUNTER
Traditional Melody

I KNOW WHAT LIES AHEAD

Words and Music by
SYLVIA JEAN CANTER

This road I'm on is straight and nar-row, but it leads to a bet-ter home. ___ It was

I SAW THE LIGHT

Words and Music by
HANK WILLIAMS

48

I WOULDN'T TAKE NOTHING
FOR MY JOURNEY NOW

Words and Music by JIMMIE DAVIS
and CHARLES F. GOODMAN

Brightly

There's noth-in' in the world that'll ev-er take the place of God's
start-ed out trav-'lin' for the Lord man-y years a-

love.
go.

Sil-ver and gold could nev-er
I've had a lot-ta heart-aches,

buy His love from a-bove.
met a lot-ta grief and woe.

When my
And

I'D RATHER BE AN OLD TIME CHRISTIAN
(Than Anything I Know)

Words and Music by
ALBERT E. BRUMLEY

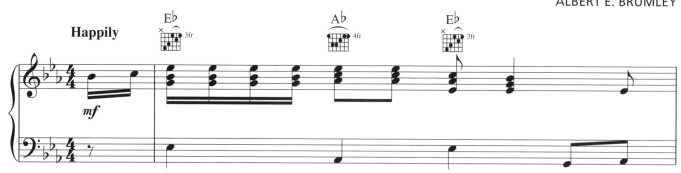

Happily

In this world I've tried most ev-'ry-thing, and I'm
man - y things I'd like to be as my
world is bright since I got right; now I

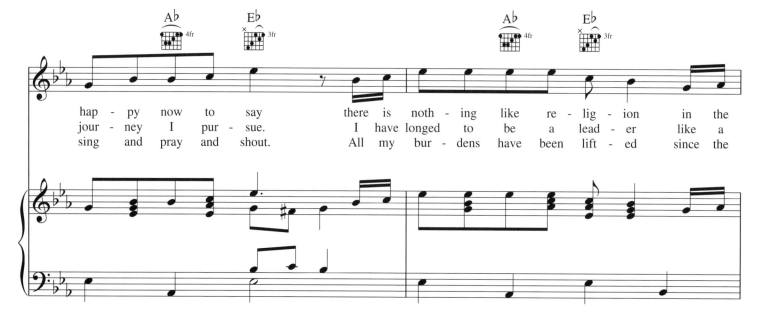

hap - py now to say
jour - ney I pur - sue.
sing and pray and shout.

there is noth - ing like re - lig - ion in the
I have longed to be a lead - er like a
All my bur - dens have been lift - ed since the

IT'S HEAVEN CALLING ME

Words and Music by MURIEL ELLIS
and JIMMIE DAVIS

Oh, I'm so glad ___ it's heav - en call - in' me. ___

There's a

D.S. al Coda

CODA

I'LL FLY AWAY

Words and Music by
ALBERT E. BRUMLEY

Verse

Some glad morn-ing when this life is o'er,____
Just a few more wea-ry days and then,____

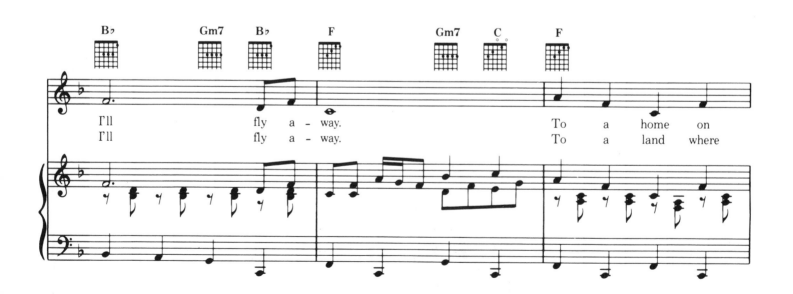

I'll fly a-way. To a home on
I'll fly a-way. To a land where

IF NOT FOR THE LOVE OF CHRIST

Words and Music by JEFF SILVEY
and TONY WOOD

Lyrics:
Look - ing back o - ver the years that I've known,___
if I had made___ this jour - ney a - lone,

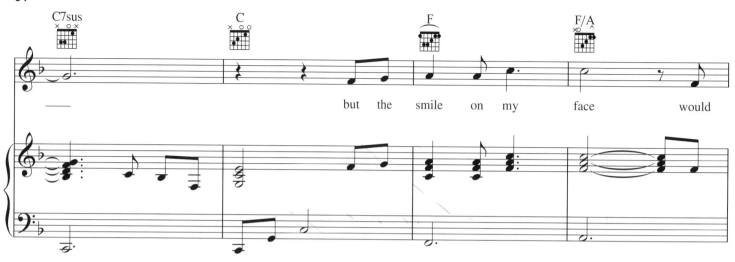

but the smile on my face would

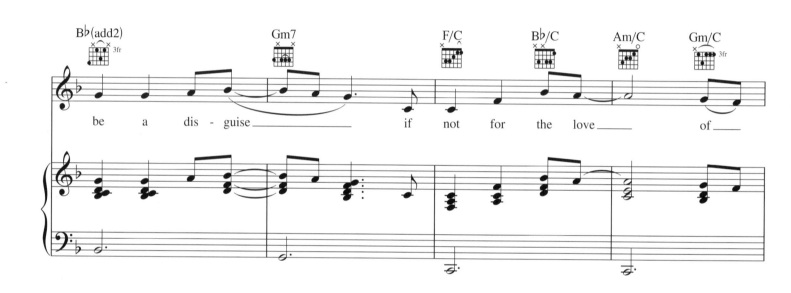

be a dis - guise _____ if not for the love _____ of _____

Christ. The love of Christ, oh, the

Christ, oh, the love _____ of Christ; _____ no fin - er treas -

- ure, no great - er prize. _____

I can't i - mag - ine _____ liv - ing my life _____ if

IT WAS JESUS

Words and Music by
JOHNNY CASH

Moderately, in 2

1. Well, a Man walked down by __ Gal - i - lee, so the Ho - ly Book does say. And a
2., 3. *(See additional lyrics)*

great mul - ti - tude was __ gath - ered there with - out a thing to eat __ for days. Up

stepped a lit - tle boy with a bas - ket. "Please take this, Lord," he said. And with

Additional Lyrics

2. Now, pay close attention, little children; it's somebody you ought to know.
It's all about a Man who walked on earth nearly two thousand years ago.
Well, He healed the sick and afflicted, and He raised them from the dead.
Then they nailed Him on an old rugged cross and put thorns on His head.
Chorus

3. Well, they took Him down and buried Him, and after the third day,
When they came to His tomb, well, they knew He was gone for the stone was rolled away.
"He's not here for He is risen," the angel of the Lord did say.
And when they saw Him walking with His nail-scarred hands they knew He came back from the dead.
Chorus

JUST A CLOSER WALK WITH THEE

Traditional
Arranged by KENNETH MORRIS

3. When my feeble life is o'er,
Time for me will be no more;
On that bright eternal shore
I will walk, dear Lord, close to Thee.

JUST A LITTLE TALK WITH JESUS

Words and Music by
CLEAVANT DERRICKS

LAND OF ISRAEL

Words and Music by
JOHN R. CASH

ON THE JERICHO ROAD

Words and Music by
DON S. McCROSSAN

LAST NIGHT I DREAMED OF HEAVEN

Words and Music by
HANK WILLIAMS

LEAD ME, FATHER

Words and Music by
JOHNNY CASH

LIFE'S RAILWAY TO HEAVEN

Words by M.E. ABBEY
Music by CHARLES D. TILLMAN

ONE MORE VALLEY

Words and Music by JIMMIE DAVIS
and DOTTIE RAMBO

(There'll Be)
PEACE IN THE VALLEY
(For Me)

Words and Music by
THOMAS A. DORSEY

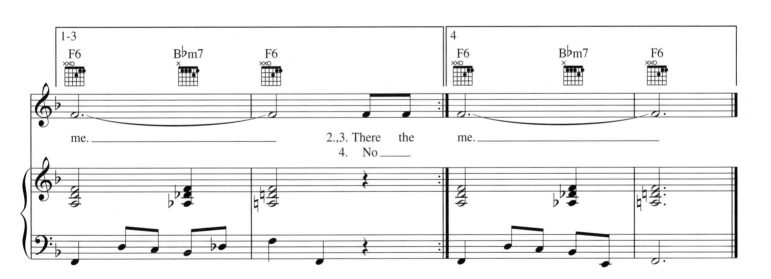

Additional Lyrics

4. No headaches or heartaches or misunderstands,
   No, confusion or trouble won't be.
   No frowns to defile, just a big endless smile,
   There'll be peace and contentment for me.
   Chorus

PRECIOUS MEMORIES

Words and Music by
J.B.F. WRIGHT

3. As I travel on life's pathway, I know not what life shall hold;
As I wander hopes grow fonder, Precious mem'ries flood my soul.

READY TO GO HOME

Words and Music by
HANK WILLIAMS

PUT YOUR HAND IN THE HAND

Words and Music by
GENE MacLELLAN

104

SAFELY IN THE ARMS OF JESUS

Words and Music by
SONNY THROCKMORTON

SHELTERED IN THE ARMS OF GOD

Words and Music by DOTTIE RAMBO
and JIMMIE DAVIS

110

SHOW ME THE WAY TO GO

Words and Music by
JEFF TWEEL

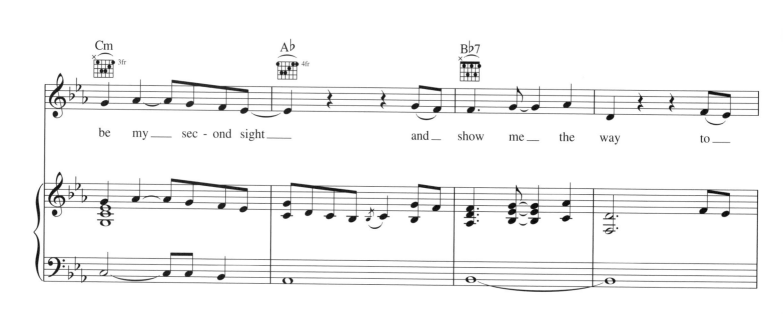

SOMEONE TO CARE

Words and Music by
JIMMIE DAVIS

Slowly, with feeling

When the world seems cold and your friends seem
dis - ap-point-ments come and you feel so

few, there is some-one who cares for you.
blue, there is some-one who cares for you.

When you've tears in your eyes, your heart bleeds in
When you need a friend, a friend till the

THIS IS JUST WHAT HEAVEN MEANS TO ME

Words and Music by
JIMMIE DAVIS

Recitation

There I'll stand on streets of gold, underneath Heaven's diamond-studded skies.
There with Jesus, where we'll never grow old, He'll wipe the tears from my weary eyes.
He'll say, "This is your mansion, son. Come on in and shake hands with dear Mother again."
And when we've all crossed over life's stormy sea, I wonder— oh, I wonder— what will it be?
Chorus

TO MY MANSION IN THE SKY

Words and Music by JIMMIE DAVIS
and JAMES W. DAVIS

TURN YOUR RADIO ON

Words and Music by
ALBERT E. BRUMLEY

THE UNCLOUDED DAY

Words and Music by
J.K. ALWOOD

WEALTH WON'T SAVE YOUR SOUL

Words and Music by
HANK WILLIAMS

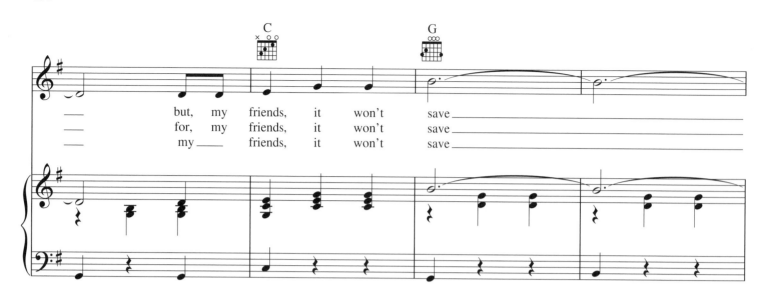

but, my friends, it won't save _____
for, my friends, it won't save _____
my _____ friends, it won't save _____

your poor wick - ed soul. _____
your poor wick - ed soul. _____
your poor wick - ed soul. _____

For when God _____
The rich man like

WILL THE CIRCLE BE UNBROKEN

Words by ADA R. HABERSHON
Music by CHARLES H. GABRIEL

WHEN THE BOOK OF LIFE IS READ

Words and Music by
HANK WILLIAMS

WHERE COULD I GO

Words and Music by
JAMES B. COATS

Verse

1. Liv - ing be - low in this old sin - ful world,
2. Neigh - bors are kind, I love them ev - 'ry one,
3. Life here is grand with friends I love so dear,

Hard - ly a com-fort can af - ford;
We get a - long in sweet ac - cord;
Com - fort I get from God's own Word;

Striv - ing a - lone to
But when my soul needs
Yet when I face the

WHO AM I

By RUSTY GOODMAN

WHY ME?
(Why Me, Lord?)

Words and Music by
KRIS KRISTOFFERSON

Moderately, with a Gospel feeling

Why me, Lord? What have I ev-er done to de-serve e-ven
If you think there's a way I can try to re-

one of the pleas-ures I've known? Tell me, Lord, What did I ev-er
pay all I've tak-en from you, May-be, Lord, I can show some-one

do that was worth lov-ing you, Or the kind-ness you've shown?
else what I've been thru my-self, On my way back to you.

WINGS OF A DOVE

Words and Music by
BOB FERGUSON

3. When Jesus went down to the waters that day,
He was baptized in the usual way.
When it was done, God blessed His Son.
He sent him His love On the wings of a dove.

THE CHRISTIAN MUSICIAN

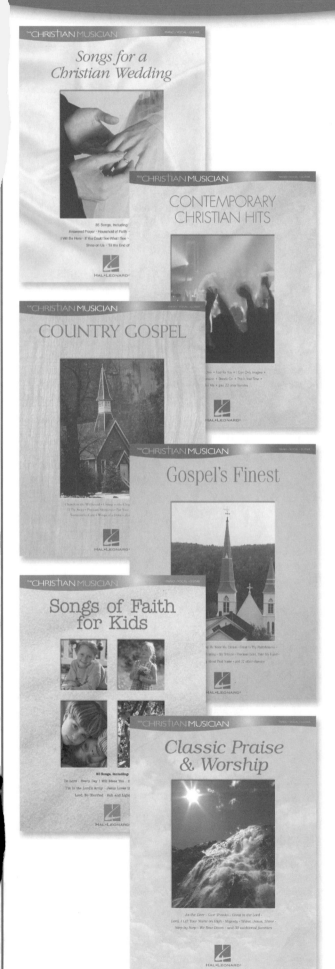

THE CHRISTIAN MUSICIAN series celebrates the many styles of music that make up the Christian faith. From Gospel favorites to today's hottest Christian artists, these books have something for all Christian musicians! There is no song duplication between any of the books!

CHRISTIAN ROCK

30 songs from today's hottest Contemporary Christian artists, including Audio Adrenaline, DC Talk, Delirious?, FFH, Jennifer Knapp, Jars of Clay, and Newsboys. Songs include: Consume Me • Everything • Flood • Get Down • Joy • One of These Days • Shine • Undo Me • and more.
00310953 Piano/Vocal/Guitar............$16.95

CLASSIC CONTEMPORARY CHRISTIAN

30 favorites essential to all Christian music repertoire, including: Arise, My Love • Awesome God • Friends • The Great Divide • His Strength Is Perfect • Love in Any Language • People Need the Lord • Where There Is Faith • and more.
00310954 Piano/Vocal/Guitar............$14.95

CLASSIC PRAISE & WORSHIP

Over 30 standards of the Praise & Worship movement, including: As the Deer • Great Is the Lord • He Is Exalted • Lord, I Lift Your Name on High • More Precious Than Silver • Oh Lord, You're Beautiful • Shine, Jesus, Shine • Step by Step • and more.
00310955 Piano/Vocal/Guitar............$14.95

CONTEMPORARY CHRISTIAN HITS

30 of today's top Christian favorites, from artists such as Avalon, Steven Curtis Chapman, DC Talk, MercyMe, Nichole Nordeman, Point of Grace, Rebecca St. James, ZOEgirl, and others. Songs include: Always Have, Always Will • Between You and Me • Can't Live a Day • Dive • Fool for You • God Is God • I Can Only Imagine • If This World • If You Want Me To • A Little More • Live Out Loud • My Will • Run to You • Steady On • Testify to Love • Wait for Me • and more.
00310952 Piano/Vocal/Guitar............$16.95

COUNTRY GOSPEL

Over 40 favorites, including: Church in the Wildwood • Crying in the Chapel • I Saw the Light • I Wouldn't Take Nothing for My Journey Now • Put Your Hand in the Hand • Turn Your Radio On • Will the Circle Be Unbroken • Wings of a Dove • and more.
00310961 Piano/Vocal/Guitar............$14.95

GOSPEL'S FINEST

Over 40 Gospel greats, including: Because He Lives • The Day He Wore My Crown • Great Is Thy Faithfulness • How Great Thou Art • In the Garden • More Than Wonderful • Precious Lord, Take My Hand • Soon and Very Soon • There's Something About That Name • and more.
00310959 Piano/Vocal/Guitar............$14.95

MODERN WORSHIP

Over 30 popular favorites of contemporary congregations, including: Above All • Ancient of Days • Breathe • The Heart of Worship • I Could Sing of Your Love Forever • It Is You • The Potter's Hand • Shout to the Lord • You Are My King (Amazing Love) • and more.
00310957 Piano/Vocal/Guitar............$14.95

SONGS FOR A CHRISTIAN WEDDING

35 songs suitable for services or receptions, including: Answered Prayer • Celebrate You • Doubly Good to You • Faithful Friend • Go There with You • Household of Faith • I Will Be Here • If You Could See What I See • My Place Is with You • Parent's Prayer (Let Go of Two) • Shine on Us • 'Til the End of Time • Where There Is Love • and more.
00310960 Piano/Vocal/Guitar............$16.95

SONGS OF FAITH FOR KIDS

50 favorites for kids of all ages! Includes: Arky, Arky • The B-I-B-L-E • Down in My Heart • God Is Bigger • He's Got the Whole World in His Hands • He's Still Workin' on Me • I'm in the Lord's Army • Lord, Be Glorified • Jesus Loves the Little Children • Salt and Light • This Little Light of Mine • Zacchaeus • and more.
00310958 Piano/Vocal/Guitar............$14.95

FOR MORE INFORMATION,
SEE YOUR LOCAL MUSIC DEALER,
OR WRITE TO:

HAL•LEONARD®
CORPORATION
7777 W. BLUEMOUND RD. P.O. BOX 13819
MILWAUKEE, WISCONSIN 53213

Visit Hal Leonard Online at
www.halleonard.com

Prices, contents, and availability subject to change without notice.

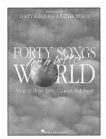

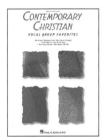

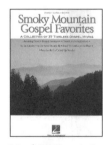